D1537980

A NOTE TO PARENTS ABOUT DISOBEYING

"Because I told you so!" is, in most cases, an insufficient motivation for children to obey their parents. Like adults, children want and need to know the rationale behind requests they are expected to fulfill.

The purpose of this book is to help children understand the basis for parental authority. In addition, it explains the importance of being obedient and tells children how to rectify situations in which they have disobeyed.

Reading and discussing this book with your child will motivate him or her to choose obedience over disobedience. It should also decrease your need to be a disciplinarian and will give you more time to be the loving, supportive parent you want to be.

Most disobedience can be avoided by making sure children know exactly what is expected of them. Disobedience can also be avoided by involving children in the formulation of the rules and regulations for which they are responsible. Children, like adults, are more willing to comply with self-imposed guidelines rather than ones that are externally imposed. Therefore, any time invested in making your child's good behavior a team effort will result in less time spent on discipline and punishment.

A Children's Book About

DISOBEYING

Managing Editor: Ellen Klarberg
Copy Editor: Annette Gooch
Editorial Assistant: Lana Eberhard
Art Director: Jennifer Wiezel
Production Artist: Gail Miller
Illustration Designer: Bartholomew
Inking Artist: Berenice Happé Iriks
Coloring Artist: Berenice Happé Iriks
Lettering Artist: Linda Hanney
Typographer: Communication Graphics

A Children's Book About

DISOBEYING

By Joy Berry

GROLIER
B O O K S

GROLIER BOOKS IS A DIVISION OF GROLIER ENTERPRISES, INC.

This book is about Annie.

Reading about Annie can help you understand and deal with **_disobeying._**

You are disobeying when you do not do what you have been told to do.

Your parents have good reasons for telling you what to do. This is why you should not disobey them.

Your parents tell you what to do because they do not want you to hurt yourself or others.

Your parents tell you what to do because they do not want you to damage or destroy things.

Your parents tell you what to do because they want you to be liked by other people.

Your parents tell you what to do because they want you to be fair.

Sometimes you might wonder why parents
get to tell their children what to do.

Parents tell their children what to do because they have lived longer and have learned more than children.

Thus, parents usually know what is best for their children.

Parents tell their children what to do because they are responsible for their children.

Parents have to take care of the damage when their children hurt themselves or others.

Sometimes parents need to punish their children for disobeying.

The purpose of a punishment is to make children feel bad about disobeying so they will not disobey again.

You can avoid being punished if you do these things:

- Talk to your parents.
- Find out what they want you to do. Then do it.

Sometimes you might not agree with your parents. Tell them how you feel.

They might change their minds. If they do not change their minds, drop the subject.

Nagging and throwing tantrums will only frustrate you and make your parents angry.

Tell the truth if you disobey.

Admit that you disobeyed.

Say that you are sorry and mean it.

Accept your punishment if you disobey.

Do not be angry at your parents when they punish you. Remember, it was you who disobeyed, not them.

Try not to disobey again.

When you obey, you please your parents,
and you are doing what is best for you.